THE SUMMER
OF MY

LITTLE
BIRD FEEDER

EDUCATIONAL NONFICTION: This is a work of nonfiction. Some parts have been simplified in varying degrees, to serve a young audience.

Book, content, and cover design by Lena Hakim. Special thanks to Camille Coates for support, Jes Marquez for initial feedback, and Richard Balthazar for edits and critique.

ISBN Number: 979-8-9850743-0-7 (Hardcover) 44 pages

Published by New Mexico Sustainably Green, a publishing platform providing environmental education materials for New Mexican youth.

For questions and feedback, please contact us at: **newmexicosustainablygreen@gmail.com**

This project is for EDUCATIONAL PURPOSES. Net proceeds donated to New Mexican avian conservation organizations.

for Camille Coates

INSTRUCTIONS FOR LIVING A LIFE.
PAY ATTENTION.
BE ASTONISHED.
TELL ABOUT IT.

Mary Oliver

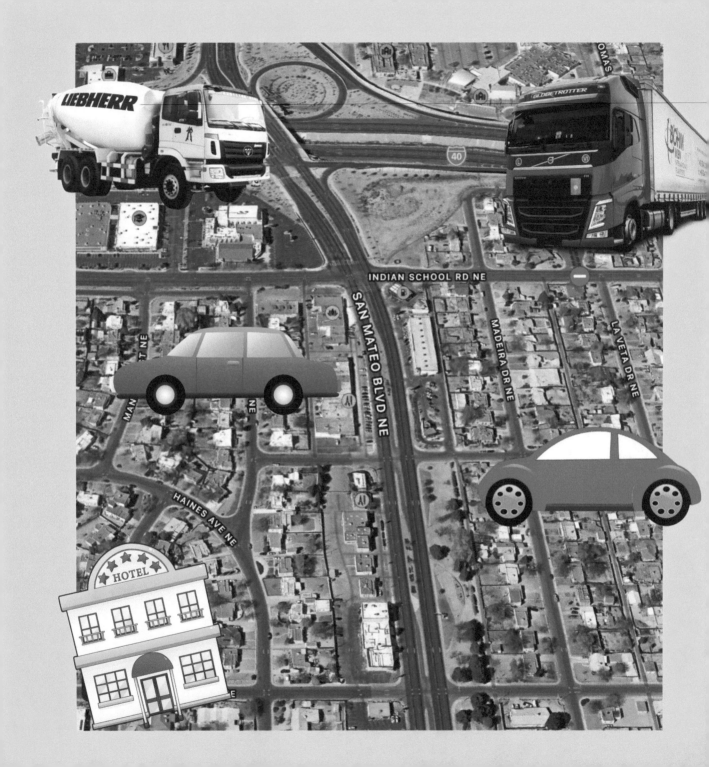

One year in early March, I moved into a home in the center of a busy city. At the end of my street was a freeway with six lanes of traffic; three going in one direction and three going the other direction. I could barely see houses and streets across the freeway.

That's my house!

OPEN

MUSCLE CAR Garage

PIZZA

I wasn't happy about the continual noise and the lack of nature, grass, and trees. There were no parks in my neighborhood, and because of the heavy traffic, walking wasn't safe. The streets in the neighborhood were filled with fast food restaurants, car repair services, and large parking lots. Here are aerial pictures of my neighborhood.

My backyard was large and hadn't been landscaped or changed. There were several trees and a few large cactus bushes called Cholla Cactus and Prickly Pear. The cacti (more than one cactus) are usually found out in the desert and on undisturbed lots within the city. In the summer pretty pink flowers appear on the Cholla Cactus, and in the fall sweet purple fruit appear on the Prickly Pear Cactus.

Cholla Cactus

Prickly Pear Cactus

Another Prickly Pear Cactus

Closeup Arial view of my backyard

There is a bird called the Curved-Bill Thrasher Which is native to the Southwest and doesn't fly much. They rely on these cacti, often foraging under them since the prickly spines offer good protection. In the winter the Thrasher eats the cactus fruit and in warmer weather bugs and seeds. I never saw the bird in my yard. I wanted to attract this bird.

This is a Cholla Cactus in the summer

This is a Curved-Bill Thrasher which I wanted to attract to my yard

This is a Prickly Pear Cactus in the winter

Birds attract other kinds of birds. So, I decided to put up a bird feeder to see what feathered friends would visit.

FINDING THE RIGHT LOCATION FOR THE BIRD FEEDER IS CRITICAL. IF THE BIRDS SEE ANYONE LOOKING AT THEM THEY'LL GET SCARED AND FLY AWAY. I HAD TO PUT THE BIRD FEEDER NEAR A WINDOW SO I COULD WATCH THEM WITHOUT THEM KNOWING. THE CACTI WERE GROWING FAR AWAY FROM MY WINDOW, SO I WOULD NEED BINOCULARS TO WATCH BIRDS VISITING CACTI.

I PUT THE BIRD FEEDER RIGHT IN FRONT OF MY KITCHEN WINDOW SO I COULD STUDY AND LEARN ABOUT ALL THE BIRDS WHO VISITED. I BOUGHT A PRE-MADE BIRD SEED MIX FROM THE STORE. AFTER SOME INVESTIGATION, I DETERMINED THESE WERE THE SEEDS IN THE MIX:

INGREDIENTS:
1.) BLACK SUNFLOWER SEEDS
2.) DRIED CORN
3.) MILLET SEEDS
4.) PEANUTS

Small birds, only 3 inches tall. They travel in pairs. Females are gray colored, and males have red heads. They have a beautiful song. I wish I could write the musical notes. ♪♪ ♪♪

Despite loud traffic sounds and few trees in the neighborhood, as soon as the bird feeder was up, birds started coming to feed. I used binoculars and looked up the type of birds (also known as "species") in books and on the computer. I took notes so I could remember what I observed about the birds: how they acted, their coloring, and their behaviors.

THE FIRST BIRDS THAT VISITED THE FEEDER ARE CALLED HOUSE FINCHES,
OR SOUTHWESTERN FINCHES. FINCHES CAN BE FOUND THROUGHOUT NORTH
AMERICA. IT WAS MARCH AND THE LEAVES ON TREES WEREN'T OUT YET.
I KNEW THEY WERE HUNGRY FROM NOT HAVING A STEADY DIET ALL WINTER.
INDEED, THEY WERE THIN. ALL DAY LONG THEY ATE THE SEEDS FROM THE FEEDER.

SOUTHWESTERN FINCHES

HOUSE SPARROWS

SOON AFTER THE FINCHES SHOWED UP, SO DID THE SPARROWS. SPARROWS ARE THE
SAME SIZE AS FINCHES, AND THEY FOLLOW FINCHES AROUND. THEY ARE NOT
FROM NORTH AMERICA, BUT RATHER EUROPE. THEIR SONGS ARE BEAUTIFUL AS WELL.

After reading that birds need water more than they need food, I immediately set up a birdbath. It was only a metal tray that I placed in the back yard. However, the birdbath attracted so many different kinds of birds!

Birds would visit in groups. The sparrows had at least eight birds in their groups. The finches had at least six birds in their groups. Dark-eyed Juncos would drink, then eat seeds which fell from the bird feeder. Spotted Towhee birds with their beautiful songs were seen but need colder weather, and headed north within two weeks.

THE NUMBER AND SPECIES OF BIRDS WERE INCREASING, AND I HAD TO KEEP UP WITH ALL THE NEW VISITORS. I STARTED DOCUMENTING THE SPECIES AND TAKING PHOTOGRAPHS.

Spotted Towhee- they appeared for two weeks. This species of bird needs colder weather, so they probably headed north.

Dark-eyed Junco- Tiny bird. Smaller than the finches. They feed only from the ground and not the elevated bird feeder.

White-winged Dove- They are the size of pigeons, but extremely shy and timid. They travel in pairs (male and female). They like the corn seeds most in the bird feeder.

PIGEONS AND STARLINGS SOON FOLLOWED THE SPARROWS INTO THE YARD. ALL THREE SPECIES OF BIRDS ARE NOT NATIVE TO NORTH AMERICA, BUT RATHER COME FROM EUROPE. THEY'RE KNOWN AS "INVASIVE SPECIES" AND LIVE IN ALMOST ALL NORTH AMERICAN CITIES. THEY CANNOT SURVIVE IN THE WILD.

FEMALE HOUSE SPARROW

MALE HOUSE SPARROW

CITY PIGEONS ARE FOUND IN ALL NORTH AMERICAN CITIES

EUROPEAN STARLINGS ARE MEAN TO NATIVE BIRDS BY PUSHING BABY OWLS, BLUEBIRDS, AND WOODPECKERS FROM THEIR NESTS

SPARROWS FOLLOW THE FINCHES AROUND. THEY LIKE TO SCARE THE FINCHES SO THAT THEY FLY AWAY

THEY FOLLOW NATIVE BIRDS AROUND AND EAT WHAT THEY EAT. MOSTLY PIGEONS SCAVENGE FOR FOOD SCRAPS, AND STARLINGS LIKE BERRIES AND INSECTS. ALL THREE BIRD SPECIES LOVE FINDING BIRD FEEDERS WITH SEEDS.

As spring turned into summer, the Cholla cacti were in full bloom. The Cholla flowers were the only flowers in the yard, and were still enough to attract hummingbirds. Occasionally a butterfly would flutter into the yard, but they didn't stay. The little hummingbirds visited the yard only while there were flowers. As soon as the flowers dropped, the hummingbirds disappeared.

Hummingbirds are tiny, and their wings move so quickly that it's hard to see them in flight

Their long beaks allow them to reach the sugary syrup within flowers (nectar). They migrate to South America in the winter, and North America in the summer

THE BACKYARD WAS QUICKLY BECOMING A MINI BIRD SANCTUARY. BIRDS FROM THE CITY CAME TO REST, DRINK, AND EAT. AS THE WEATHER WARMED, EVEN MORE SPECIES OF BIRDS SHOWED UP. HOWEVER, SO TOO DID BIRDS WHICH HUNT OTHER BIRDS. CATS FROM THE NEIGHBORHOOD LURKED IN THE BUSHES.

THIS IS A ROADRUNNER. THEY EAT BUGS, LIZARDS, AND SMALL BIRDS. THEY DON'T FLY. THEY HOP AND RUN FAST.

HOW THIS BIRD FOUND MY BACK YARD WITH ALL THE HIGHWAYS AND TRAFFIC IS A MYSTERY!

THE BIRD FEEDER WAS TOO SMALL FOR SO MANY VISITING BIRDS.
I STARTED SPRINKLING SEEDS ON THE PATIO IN THE BACK YARD. THE
ROADRUNNER WOULD HIDE NEAR A CACTUS, AND THE SPARROWS WOULD
PERCH IN THE TREE NEXT DOOR.

One morning, while putting more seeds out on the patio, I noticed another roadrunner sitting on the fence. There were now two roadrunners. They weren't interested in the Finches, only the sparrows that came down to eat. They continually watched them.

Suddenly, there was a commotion. It was fast. The roadrunners ran towards the sparrows who came down to eat seeds on the patio. I heard a scream from a sparrow. When I looked up, the sparrows were in the air and heading towards the neighbor's tree.

As the sparrows hid in the tree, I heard the most unusual sound come from them. It wasn't a song, but a communal moaning that I'd never heard before. That's when I realized the roadrunner had hunted and caught a sparrow. The sound the rest of the sparrows made might be a mourning cry for their lost family member. I couldn't find verification in books, so I noted the observation in my bird journal.

EVERY DAY THE ROADRUNNERS WOULD WALK THROUGH THE YARD. THERE WERE TWO, BUT ONCE I COUNTED THREE! I REALIZED THE CONTINUAL PRESENCE OF ROADRUNNERS KEPT THE CITY PIGEONS AND STARLINGS AWAY. THE SPARROWS REMAINED AFRAID AND ALWAYS STAYED IN THE TREE UNTIL THE COAST WAS CLEAR OF ROADRUNNERS.

ROADRUNNERS PATROLLED THE YARD! THE SHY WHITE-WINGED DOVES WOULD COME TO FEED REGULARLY. THEY SELDOM TRAVEL IN GROUPS, BUT THE SAFETY OF THE YARD ALLOWED THEM TO COME IN LARGE NUMBERS. THE YARD WAS NOW A REFUGE FOR NATIVE BIRDS!

ROADRUNNER ON PATROL!

WHITE-WINGED DOVES AND MOURNING DOVES WOULD EAT THE SEEDS ON THE GROUND. THEY ARE TOO BIG FOR THE BIRD FEEDER, BUT THEY TRIED!

IN THE EARLY SUMMER MONTHS, I NOTICED A MALE CURVED-BILL THRASHER IN A CACTUS! I DON'T KNOW HOW HE FOUND THE YARD OR HAD RELOCATED DURING THE WINTER MONTHS AND NOW RETURNED. HE NEVER ATE ANY SEEDS, BUT CONTINUALLY SCRATCHED AND DUG FOR FOOD UNDER THE CACTUS BUSHES. DURING THE DAY HE STAYED HIDDEN, BUT SOMETIMES HE JUMPED ONTO BRANCHES OR THE FENCE.

I CALLED HIM "MR. THRASHER"

EVERY EVENING FOR TWO WEEKS MR. THRASHER WENT UP THE TREE AND SANG HIS MATING CALL. EACH EVENING HIS CALL BECAME STRONGER AND LOUDER. IT WENT ON LONGER, SOMETIMES UNTIL MIDNIGHT. NO FEMALE THRASHER APPEARED. I KNEW HOW DESPERATE HE WAS BECOMING, AND I WAS SAD HE WASN'T ABLE TO FIND A MATE.

EXACTLY TWO WEEKS LATER, MR. THRASHER STOPPED CALLING AND LEFT THE YARD. I COULDN'T FIND HIM ANYWHERE. THIS UPSET ME.

From dawn until dusk, birds visited the yard. They drank from the birdbath and ate the seeds. As the roadrunners continued to patrol the yard, fewer sparrows came to the feeder. The songs of native birds could be heard all day, and I learned to identify what sounds belonged to which species of bird.

I missed Mr. Thrasher as he was the main species of bird I wanted to attract, but he was gone. I continued to make observations. Here are pictures of the wildlife and bird species I saw in the yard.

Can you identify these birds?

AFTER AN ENTIRE MONTH, MR. THRASHER CAME BACK TO THE YARD! HE BROUGHT BACK A FEMALE THRASHER. OF ALL THE CACTI IN THE CITY, WITH ALL THE TRAFFIC OBSTACLES TO REACH THE YARD, HE CAME BACK TO MY YARD!

ALL DAY LONG, THE ROADRUNNERS WATCHED OVER THE YARD.

THAT'S MR. THRASHER! HE CAME BACK AND BROUGHT A FEMALE THRASHER WITH HIM!

THAT'S THE FEMALE CURVED-BILL THRASHER THAT MR. THRASHER BROUGHT BACK. SHE IS SMALLER IN SIZE, AND DOESN'T VENTURE FAR FROM HER CACTUS.

MR. AND MS. THRASHER NEVER LEFT THE YARD AGAIN

I CALLED HER "MS. THRASHER"

Mr. and Ms. Thrasher were comfortable in their cacti. The pigeons, sparrows, and starlings seldom visited the yard. The roadrunners continued to patrol the neighborhood.

I DID IT!
IN THE MIDDLE OF THE BUSY CITY,
IN MY OWN BACK YARD,
I CREATED A NATIVE BIRD SANCTUARY!

As summer ended and the seasons changed,
so too did the birds that visited the feeder. The roadrunners left the
yard to go south for warmer weather. As soon as the roadrunners were gone,
the sparrows returned, as did the pigeons. The only native species that stayed
were the finches and Thrashers.

The summer of my little bird feeder was a success. I created a mini backyard
sanctuary for native birds. I'm going to share with you how you can create
a bird sanctuary and become a naturalist, all in your own back yard!

How to start your own backyard bird sanctuary And become a naturalist

1.) Find out which birds are native to your area. This can be done by contacting your neighborhood library and asking for books and resources on local birds. It can be done by contacting the Audubon Society in your area and asking for resources and classes. Ask parents and teachers, and call your City Environmental offices too.

2.) Set up a birdbath. All birds need water. even if you're not going to put up a bird feeder, birds will visit if there is fresh, clean water in a bowl in the yard. Change out the water daily, especially if a lot of birds visit your birdbath. If you live in a desert environment, always have water available for birds.

3.) FIND OUT WHAT KIND OF SEEDS THE BIRDS IN YOUR AREA EAT. MOST PLACES THAT SELL SEED MIXES WILL PROVIDE THE RIGHT FOODS FOR THE BIRDS IN YOUR AREA. TAKE THE TIME TO LEARN ABOUT THE DIETS OF YOUR VISITING BIRDS.

MIGRATORY BIRDS LIKE MILLET AND PEANUTS

SOUTHWESTERN BIRDS LIKE CORN

ALL BIRDS LIKE SUNFLOWER SEEDS

4.) FILL A BIRD FEEDER WITH SEEDS. PUT IT IN A TREE OR SOMEWHERE ABOVE THE GROUND. YOU MAY HAVE TO RELOCATE THE FEEDER SEVERAL TIMES UNTIL YOU FIND A LOCATION WHERE THE BIRDS CAN SAFELY EAT THE SEEDS WHILE YOU WATCH THEM.

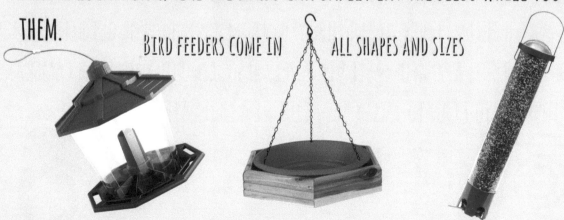

BIRD FEEDERS COME IN   ALL SHAPES AND SIZES

You can buy bird feeders from the store, or you can make them from plastic bottles. Try not to use metal bird feeders. They get hot in the sun and can burn their feet. Putting seeds in an open tray works too, but it should be well above the ground so squirrels and mice can't reach the seeds.

5.) Birds are often scared of people. Set the bird feeder well away from where you will watch them. Either watch the birds from a window or get binoculars to watch them from a comfortable distance. Also, consider using a camera to take pictures so you can identify the birds at a later time.

6.) Keep a bird journal on the species that come to your yard. Learn to recognize individuals. All birds have unique features and coloring. Pay attention to their differences.

Mr. Thrasher?
Is that you?

Start noting how many birds of a certain species visit your yard. Invasive bird species (e.g. pigeons and sparrows) may be the only birds that show up to your feeder for a long time. Keep watching out for native birds. This is why being observant is critical. When the right plants are available, native species will visit (see #9).

Counted 3 different roadrunners

Saw 5 hummingbirds

There are too many sparrows to count!

7.) FIND A WAY TO KEEP CATS AND OTHER PREDATORS AWAY FROM THE BIRD FEEDER. THE GROUND AT THE BOTTOM OF THE FEEDER SHOULD BE CLEAR OF BUSHES AND HIDING PLACES FOR OTHER ANIMALS.

8.) IT'S IMPORTANT TO FEED HUMMINGBIRDS. TODAY, ALL HUMMINGBIRD SPECIES ARE NOT DOING WELL BECAUSE THERE ARE NOT ENOUGH FLOWERS IN THE WILD. THEY ONLY EAT THE SUGAR SYRUP FOUND IN FLOWERS CALLED NECTAR. THEY DON'T EAT SEEDS OR DRINK WATER. TO HELP THEM, YOU CAN MAKE A SUGAR SOLUTION AND POUR IT INTO A SPECIAL HUMMINGBIRD FEEDER. OR BETTER YET, MAKE CERTAIN YOUR YARD HAS FLOWERING PLANTS WHICH ARE "POLLINATOR FRIENDLY." THIS MEANS THEY ARE THE EXACT FLOWERS WHICH HUMMINGBIRDS AND BEES EAT.

IF I HAD MORE FLOWERS IN MY YARD HUMMINGBIRDS, BEES AND BUTTERFLIES WOULD HAVE STAYED LONGER.

HUMMINGBIRD FEEDERS CAN BE HUNG IN ANY TREE.
THEY WILL ATTRACT OTHER
HUNGRY POLLINATORS,
SUCH AS BUTTERFLIES
AND BEES.

Hummingbird Solution:
1 Part White sugar to 3 parts pure water. Mix until sugar is dissolved. Pour into Hummingbird Feeder.

Wash and rinse the feeder every three days. Then add more fresh sugar solution.

THE BEST FOODS FOR HUMMINGBIRDS ARE NATIVE FLOWERING PLANTS, GRASSES AND CACTI. THEY CONTAIN NECTAR, WHICH HUMMINGBIRDS DRINK DAILY.

9.) The most important thing you can do to attract birds is to know which type of plant the bird lives inside or on, then grow those plants. Some plants produce flowers which hummingbirds drink. Some plants attract bugs which bird eats. Some plants provide both.

It might be impossible to grow a certain tree or plant. They don't have to be in your yard, but they need to be nearby to attract the bird.

If you are in the Southwest, grasses are important because many produce flowers and hold moisture in the soil, allowing bugs to survive. Cacti are home to lizards, bugs, and birds, so include them in your yard.

10.) There are common words used when studying birds. Here is a short list of words you should learn and understand:

- **Audubon** - Someone who studies birds

- **Avian** - A bird, or birds

- **Ecosystem** - A community of plants and animals that rely upon each other to survive

- **Environment** - total, or part, of the natural world

- **Habitat** - The Home of a plant or animal

- **Indigenous** - Another word for 'Native.' They are naturally from that place

-  **Invasive** - A plant, animal, or bird that doesn't belong there, or comes from somewhere else

☑ **NATIVE-** A PLANT, ANIMAL, OR BIRD THAT BELONGS THERE, AND COMES FROM THAT PLACE

☑ **NATURALIST-** SOMEONE WHO WATCHES AND STUDIES NATURE

☑ **NECTAR-** SWEET, NUTRITIOUS SYRUP FOUND IN FLOWERING PLANTS. POLLINATORS (BIRDS, BEES AND BUTTERFLIES) FEED ON NECTAR

☑ **POLLINATORS-** BIRDS, BUTTERFLIES, MOTHS, WASPS, AND BEES ARE POLLINATORS. THEY VISIT FLOWERS TO FEED ON NECTAR OR POLLEN IN THE FLOWER

☑ **PREDATORS-** AN ANIMAL THAT HUNTS ANOTHER ANIMAL

☑ **SPECIES-** THE SAME TYPE OF PLANT, ANIMAL, OR BIRD. MR. THRASHER IS OF THE SPECIES 'CURVED BILL THRASHERS'

HAPPY BIRD WATCHING!

Lena Hakim is an environmental scientist and passionate naturalist for high desert ecosystems. She loves watching and studying prairie dogs and native birds in her home town. She hopes this book inspires young people to look closer at all nature in their neighborhoods, and work to protect all wildlife.

This project was designed as a fundraiser for New Mexico's avian conservation organizations. 100% of net proceeds will be donated to them. This project isn't affiliated with the National Audubon Society (NAS) or its divisions, though donations will be made to Audubon New Mexico. Copies of this book will be donated to their children's school for direct fundraising and classes.